2/2/12

W9-BVU-355

Looking at Landforms

Ellen K. Mitten

ROURKE PUBLISHING

Vero Beach, Florida 32964

www.rourkepublishing.com

PHOTO CREDITS: © Karyn Kudrna: Title Page; © Natalia Bratslavesky: 3, 23; © Jan Rysavy: 4, 21; © Kris Hanke: 5, 23; © Sheldon Kralstein: 7; © Darien Nordling: 9; © David Ciemny: 11; © Jamie Roset: 13; © photo75: 15; © S. Greg Panosian: 15; © Pathathai Chungyam: 17; © Andrew David: 19; © Xiaoping Liang: 21: © Ian Cumberland: 21

Edited by Meg Greve

Cover design by Nicola Stratford bppublishing.com
Interior design by Tara Raymo

Library of Congress Cataloging-in-Publication Data

Mitten, Ellen.
  Looking at landforms / Ellen K. Mitten.
     p. cm. -- (Little world Geography)
  ISBN 978-1-60694-421-9 (hard cover)
  ISBN 978-1-60694-537-7 (soft cover)
  1. Landforms--Juvenile literature. I. Title.
  GB401.5.M58 2010
  551.41--dc22
                                    2009005745

Printed in the USA

CG/CG

ROURKE PUBLISHING

www.rourkepublishing.com - rourke@rourkepublishing.com
Post Office Box 643328 Vero Beach, Florida 32964

What are **landforms?**

Landforms are the bumps and grooves on the **surface** of the **Earth**.

5

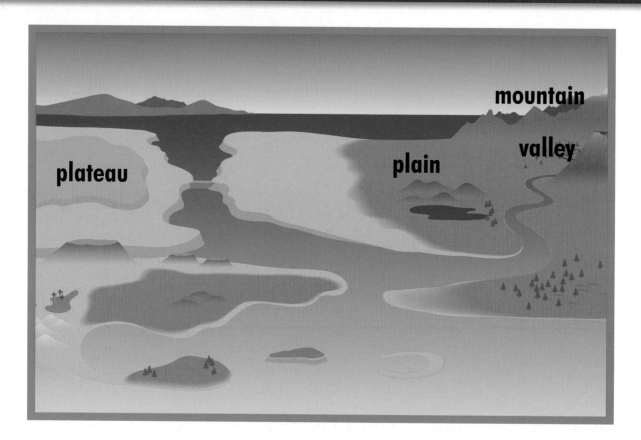

The Earth's surface is bumpy because of mountains, valleys, **plateaus**, and plains.

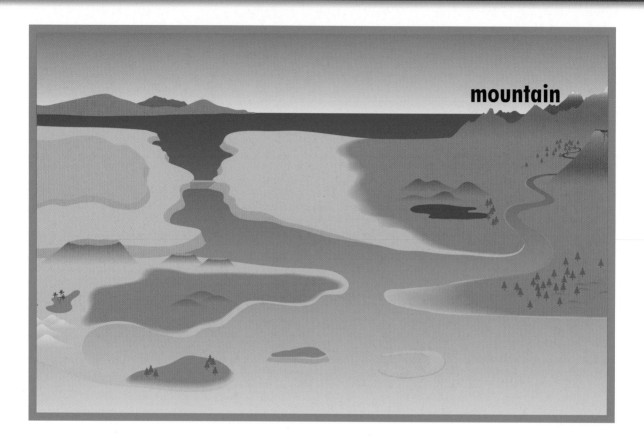

Mountains are the world's tallest landform.

Mountains are found on all seven **continents**. The tallest mountain of all is Mount Everest.

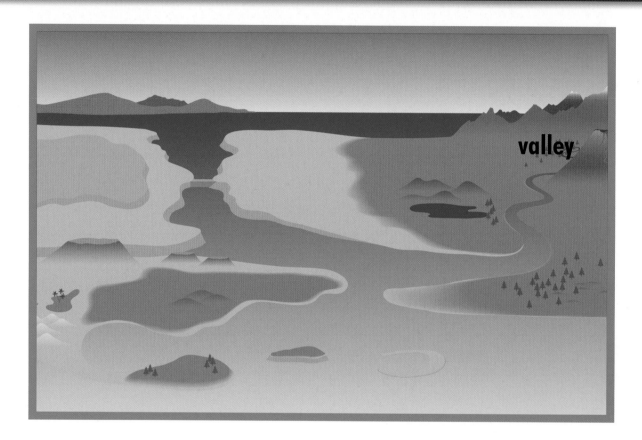

valley

Valleys are the low places of land found between mountains.

Valleys can be made by rivers or by **glaciers**.

Rivers make "V" shaped valleys.

Glaciers make "U" shaped valleys.

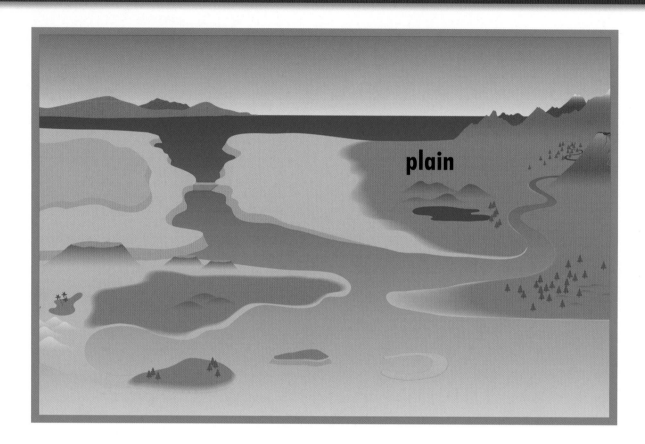

Flat, low land is called a plain.

Plains are found in the center of a continent. Plains take many years to form and are very old.

Plateaus are areas of high, flat land. What landforms are around you?

The Tibetan Plateau is the highest plateau on Earth.

GLOSSARY

 **continents** (KON-tuh-nuhnts): The largest land masses on Earth. They are Asia, Africa, Europe, North America, South America, Australia, and Antarctica.

 **Earth** (URTH): The planet on which we live. Earth is the third planet from the Sun, between Venus and Mars.

 **glaciers** (GLAY-shurs): Huge layers of ice found between mountains. Most glaciers do not melt because the temperature does not go over freezing in the areas where they can be found.

landforms (LAND-forms): The features of the surface of the Earth, such as mountains, valleys, plateaus, and plains.

plateaus (pla-TOHZ): Areas of high, flat land.

surface (SUR-fiss): The outside layer of the Earth that we can see. The Earth's surface contains landforms and water, such as oceans, rivers, and lakes.

Index

Websites to Visit

www.enchantedlearning.com/geography/landforms/glossary.shtml

www.kidsgeo.com

www.nps.gov/brca/forkids/landformskids.htm

About the Author

Ellen K. Mitten has been teaching four and five-year-olds since 1995. She and her family love reading all sorts of books!

It's About Time!™

All About an Hour

Joanne Randolph

PowerKiDS
press
New York

Published in 2008 by The Rosen Publishing Group, Inc.
29 East 21st Street, New York, NY 10010

First Edition

Book Design: Kate Laczynski
Photo Researcher: Nicole Pristash

Photo Credits: Cover, pp. 1, 22 © www.istockphoto.com/Clayton Hansen; p. 4 © SuperStock, Inc.; p. 6 © www.istockphoto.com/Soubrette; pp. 8, 10, 12, 18, 20 © Shutterstock.com; p. 14 © www.istockphoto.com/stocksnapper; p. 16 © Peter Dazeley/Getty Images; p. 24 © www.istockphoto.com/René Mansi.

Library of Congress Cataloging-in-Publication Data

Randolph, Joanne.
  All about an hour / Joanne Randolph. — 1st ed.
      p. cm. — (It's about time!)
  Includes index.
  ISBN-13: 978-1-4042-3766-7 (library binding)
  ISBN-10: 1-4042-3766-6 (library binding)
  1. Time—Miscellanea—Juvenile literature. 2. Clocks and watches—Miscellanea—Juvenile literature. I. Title.
  QB209.5.R36 2008
  529'.2—dc22
                                        2006036618

Manufactured in the United States of America

Contents

What is an hour? Let's find out.

It's what this book is all about.

Each day has 12 hours. Each night has 12, too.

That's 24 hours for time to pass through.

Twelve o'clock in the day
is called midday or noon.

When this hour comes, we
know it will be lunchtime soon.

Midnight comes at twelve o'clock, too, but this time it's at night.

In our soft, warm beds, we are snuggled tight.

We use the hours to help us through our day.

They tell us when to catch the bus and when it's time to play.

Look at this clock. What's on its face?

Twelve numbers name the hours. Two hands set the pace.

The short hand on the clock counts the hours as they go.

What hour does the short hand on this clock show?

Some clocks do not use hands to tell the time of day.

They use numerals instead. What time does this clock say?

Your school play lasts one hour, and it's three o'clock right now.

What time will it be when you take your bow?

Ticktock, ticktock, telling time is fun.

You can count the hours in the day, and now our book is done!

Key to the Hours

twelve o'clock

one o'clock

two o'clock

three o'clock

four o'clock

five o'clock

six o'clock

seven o'clock

eight o'clock

nine o'clock

ten o'clock

eleven o'clock

Index

Web Sites

Due to the changing nature of Internet links, PowerKids Press has developed an online list of Web sites related to the subject of this book. This site is updated regularly. Please use this link to access the list: www.powerkidslinks.com/iat/hour/

24